Short Course

Bryan Coombs

PITMAN PUBLISHING
128 Long Acre, London WC2E 9AN

© Sir Isaac Pitman Limited 1986

First published in Great Britain 1986
Reprinted 1986, 1987

British Library Cataloguing in Publication Data
Coombs, Bryan
   Pitman 2000 shorthand: a short course.
   1. Shorthand—Pitman—Examinations, questions, etc.
   I. Title
   653'.4242'076   256.2.P5

Text set in 11 on 16 pt Univers Light
Printed and bound in Great Britain

ISBN 0 273 02324 1

Contents

Acknowledgements

The author wishes to express his appreciation to Betty Ball and Margaret Brown who read through each stage of the manuscript. Their expert advice was invaluable and was of great assistance in writing the book.

Special thanks, too, to my editor, Pam Wickham, for her masterful handling of this demanding task, from the early days of general discussion to the final production.

Study Plan

The activities described should take place daily:

1 DRILLING* (Theory examples)

Drill each theory example until mastered. This repetitive writing of an outline assists in mastering. Keep in mind the aim of drilling and never allow it to become dull. It is important to build up a vocabulary of frequently used outlines.

* Drilling is the writing of an outline many times until you are confident that whenever you hear that outline again in dictation, you will never have any hesitancy in writing. The first time you write an outline write it carefully, and get the feel of it, but at each repetition write faster and faster. As you write say the word(s) to yourself. This is your own personal dictation system and is invaluable and keeps the drilling meaningful.

2 READING (Progress Checks, Reading and Writing, Dictation)

Read each passage several times and aim to read the outlines as quickly as if the passage was typescript. The aim of this reading is to develop a rapid reading skill. This can only come through instant recognition of each outline. This skill transfers to the writing skill. Rapid reading develops rapid writing.

Rapid-read each Dictation Passage either by way of pre-dictation preparation, or as a remedial procedure in between each dictation. Reading is an easy way to develop your shorthand skill; push your reading speed of shorthand as high as your ordinary reading speed.

3 DICTATION (Progress Checks, Reading and Writing, Dictation)

Each Progress Check and Dictation Passage must be taken from live or recorded dictation. To be of any value the dictation must be repeated at least three times. This repetition is one of the key factors in skill building.

After each dictation some form of remedial work must take place before repeating the dictation. Read back your notes. Check outlines and encircle errors; drill each correction and any outlines which caused hesitancy. Rapid-read the shorthand passage. Then take the repeat dictation. This remedial work takes place in between each dictation. The correction of errors allows progress to take place.

4 TYPEWRITTEN TRANSCRIPTION

If you are already able to type you should begin transcription training in Unit 1 by typing each shorthand passage. Transcribe your own shorthand notes on the typewriter. You may find your speed is slow at first but this will improve as you gain confidence in the writing and transcribing of the shorthand.

If you are just learning to type you should begin typing back your notes as soon as you have mastered the keyboard. Typewritten transcription is the only form of transcription in the business world and therefore skill should be developed from the earliest possible moment!

When transcribing memoranda and letters, remember to display these correctly.

The Consonants

*With the exception of **w, y** and the aspirate **h,** the strokes representing the consonant sounds are derived from the simple geometrical structures shown in the following diagrams:*

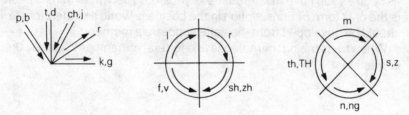

The following is an analysis of the diagrams:

Straight downstrokes

p   b   t   d   ch   j

Curved downstrokes

f   v   th   TH   s   z   sh   zh   r

Straight horizontal strokes

k   g

Curved horizontal strokes

m   n   ng

Straight upstroke

r

Curved upstroke

l

Specially formed upstrokes

w   y   h

Unit 1
Strokes P, B, T, D, CH, J; heavy dot vowels

Pitman Shorthand is written according to sound ie it is phonetic. For example the shorthand symbols for the words **draught** *and* **draft** *are exactly the same because the words are sounded the same.*

Words are made up of consonants and vowels. Consonants eg **P, B** *are represented by strokes and are written thin or thick. Thin strokes eg* ╲ **P,** *represent light sounds, and thick strokes eg* ╲ **B,** *heavy sounds. Vowels are represented by light or heavy dots and dashes; light for light sounds eg* **e** *as in* **bet,** *and heavy for heavy sounds eg* **ay** *as in* **pay.** *The formation of strokes and vowels which represents a word is called an* **outline.**

Straight Strokes

P ╲ *B* ╲ *T* | *D* | *CH* ╱ *J* ╱

Strokes may be written in different positions in relation to the line, called first, second and third position:

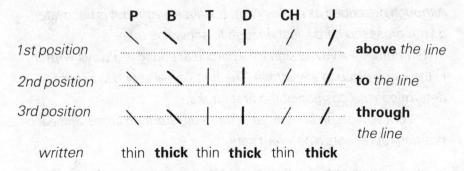

	P	B	T	D	CH	J	
1st position	╲	╲	|	|	╱	╱	**above** *the line*
2nd position	╲	╲	|	|	╱	╱	**to** *the line*
3rd position	╲	╲	|	|	╱	╱	**through** *the line*
written	thin	**thick**	thin	**thick**	thin	**thick**	

Practise writing these strokes in the three positions. Just touch the paper with your pen/pencil when writing the thin strokes and add only the slightest extra pressure to write the thick strokes. The size of your shorthand outlines should be approximately the same as those shown in this book.

Strokes and Vowels

Each vowel sound is represented by a sign and the sign for a particular sound is **always** written in the same position in relation to any stroke. Each vowel sound is classified as either a 1st place, 2nd place or 3rd place vowel. It never changes. The sound **ah** as in **Pa** is always a 1st place vowel and is always placed at the beginning of a stroke .... **Pa.** The first vowel sound in a word decides the position of the first up or down stroke. In the word **Pa** the first sound is **ah,** a first place vowel, so the stroke is written above the line, first position, and the vowel put in the first place ....

Heavy Dot Vowels

The first vowel sign you are going to work with is a heavy dot. Although described as a heavy dot, because a light dot is used later, do not press too hard—just enough to show it is there.

Remember—a vowel sign for a particular sound is always written in the same place to any stroke. The first vowel sound in a word determines the position of the first stroke.

The dot vowel can be written in three different positions and each position represents a different sound:

a   at the beginning of a stroke, 1st place representing **ah**   Pa.
When the first vowel is 1st place the first stroke is written above the line

b *in the middle of a stroke, 2nd place representing* **ay** ⟍ **pay.**
*When the first vowel is 2nd place the first stroke is written to
the line*

c *at the end of a stroke, 3rd place representing* **ee** ⟍. **pea.**
*When the first vowel is 3rd place the first stroke is written through
the line*

*In the following examples the vowel is pronounced after the
consonant and the dot is placed to the right of the stroke.* **Always
write the stroke first and then add the vowel.**

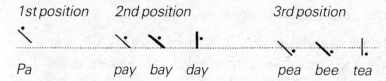

1st position	2nd position			3rd position		
Pa	pay	bay	day	pea	bee	tea

*Write each of the examples several times. The first time you write
an outline you might be a little slow. Aim to speed up your writing
until you can write each one very quickly before moving to the next
example.*

*When pronounced before a straight downstroke the dot is placed
to the left. Remember to write the stroke first and then add the
vowel:*

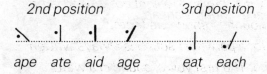

2nd position				3rd position	
ape	ate	aid	age	eat	each

Drill each outline until you feel confident that you know each one.

Joined Strokes

1 *Strokes may be joined. The position of the first stroke is
determined by the first vowel sound in the word. The second*

stroke is simply joined to the first. Remember that the direction of a stroke never changes. Complete the joined strokes as one movement, avoiding any hesitancy where the strokes meet. This ease of movement comes with practice. After completing the joined strokes add the vowel:

page   bait   tape   date

Drill the examples: As soon as you reach the line with the first stroke, immediately write the second stroke; the joined strokes are written quickly and as a single movement.

2 When two strokes are joined and the first vowel is a 3rd place vowel, as in **beat,** the first downstroke is written through the line, but the vowel is placed in the third position **before** the second stroke. This results in positive vowel indication. In the outline **cheap,** if the 3rd place vowel **ee** was written at the end of the **CH** it would not be clear whether it was in fact a 3rd place vowel to the **CH** or a 1st place vowel to the **P.**

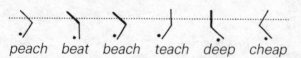

peach   beat   beach   teach   deep   cheap

Short Forms

Frequently occurring words are represented by abbreviated outlines. Several are introduced in each unit and it is important to master them immediately by drilling, that is writing each one many times and saying the word to yourself as you write rapidly. The importance of these outlines cannot be overstressed. Nine of these very simple words represent 25% of all business and general dictation. Short forms must be learned thoroughly.

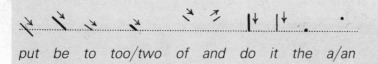

| put | be | to | too/two | of | and | do | it | the | a/an |

Punctuation

1 *A full stop is written with a single movement* ....
   A question mark is written ....
   An exclamation mark ....
2 *Two small upward dashes underneath an outline denote a proper noun,* .... **Jay,** *or any word requiring an initial capital letter.*

Progress Checks

These exercises appear in each unit throughout the book and should be used to consolidate theory knowledge up to that particular point.
Read the sentences. If you have any problem reading an outline do not refer to the key but rather work again through the theory points which have just been presented and this will provide the information you need. Re-read the sentences and then copy them into your notebook. Look at an outline, absorb it and then write it quickly. Shorthand notes are always written quickly and accurately.

Progress Check 1.1

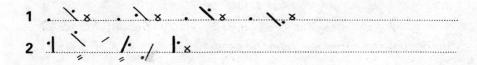

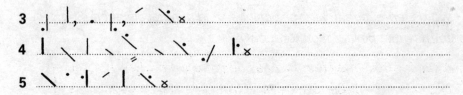

6

3 ....

4 ....

5 ....

Phrases

1 *Without lifting your pen/pencil it is possible to join two or more outlines together to form phrases. Phrases are easy and quick to write and should be used as often as possible.* Practise and master the phrases as you meet them.

Write the first word of a phrase in the correct position:

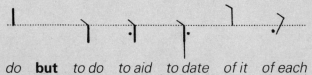

do   **but**   to do   to aid   to date   of it   of each

2 *Another way to represent* **the** *is to add a tick to the end of an outline and write it as a phrase. You may write the tick upwards or downwards, whichever forms the sharper angle, and the tick goes down after strokes* **P** *and* **B**, *and up after strokes* **T** *and* **D**. *Writing* **the** *this way is faster and is also easier to read back:*

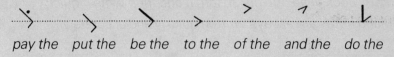

pay the   put the   be the   to the   of the   and the   do the

3 *The short form* .. *for* **the** *is always used when* **the** *begins a sentence:*

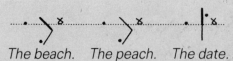

The beach.   The peach.   The date.

Intersections

A single stroke may represent a complete word when intersected into or written close to another outline. The first intersection is ⌐↓ **department.**

each department

Progress Check 1.2

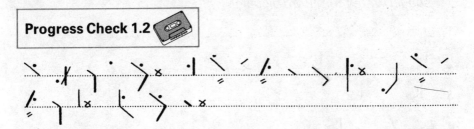

Vowel Review

A full understanding of the vowels is essential for progress and therefore a vowel review will be a part of the first four units. Drill the outlines which follow and make absolutely sure that you are confident about how to write these outlines before leaving this section. Always write the stroke(s) first and then add the vowel.

heavy dot vowel

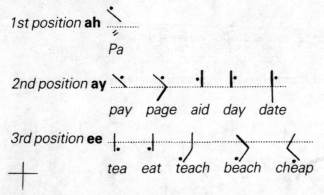

1st position **ah**

Pa

2nd position **ay**

pay   page   aid   day   date

3rd position **ee**

tea   eat   teach   beach   cheap

Reading and Writing Practice

- Aim to read each shorthand sentence as quickly as if it was typescript.
- Any outline which causes you to hesitate should be checked in the key and then drilled.
- Re-read the sentences trying to increase your speed.
- When you can read the sentences without any hesitation you should write them from dictation.

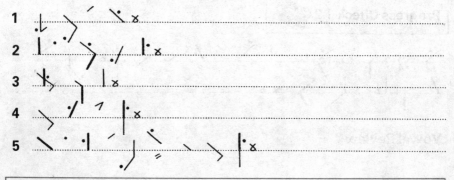

Dictation

- Read and then rapid-read each passage of shorthand several times.
- Prepare for dictation by drilling the shorthand outlines until you know you will be able to write each outline from dictation without any hesitancy.
- Take each passage from dictation several times.
- After each dictation, check outlines and drill any corrections before repeating the dictation. This remedial work is essential and ensures progress.

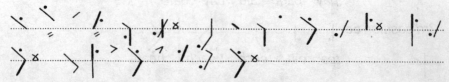

Unit 2
Heavy dash vowels; strokes K, G, M

Heavy Dash Vowels

There are three more heavy vowels, represented by a heavy dash:

1st position   **aw** *as in* **jaw**
2nd position   **o** *as in* **Joe**
3rd position   **ōō** *as in* **chew**

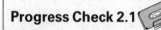

jaw paw bought oat tow boat obey chew bōot

Progress Check 2.1

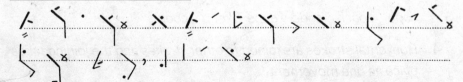

Horizontal Strokes

1   *Horizontal strokes (straight or curved) are written from left to right
and when alone are placed above the line for 1st position, and
on the line for 2nd and 3rd position:*

	K	G	M
1st position	→	⇒	⌣
2nd position			
3rd position			
written	thin	**thick**	thin

> **Note**   *Stroke* **M** *is a shallow, scooped-out curve.*

9

2 *When a vowel is sounded first it is written above a horizontal stroke, and when it is sounded after, it is written below. Remember, write the stroke(s) first and then the vowel:*

1st position
calm

2nd position
ache   go   aim   may   game   make

3rd position
eke   key   me

3 *When an outline begins with a horizontal stroke and is followed by a downstroke, it is the downstroke which is placed in the correct position according to the first sounded vowel:*

cope   coach   code   gape   keep   coop

4 *Horizontal strokes are joined to other strokes and the joining takes place as one movement.*

Remember that when two strokes are joined and the first vowel is 3rd place, the first downstroke is written through the line, but the vowel is placed in the third position **before** *the second stroke.*

beam   boom   teak   team   deep   deem   talk   take   chalk

Progress Check 2.2

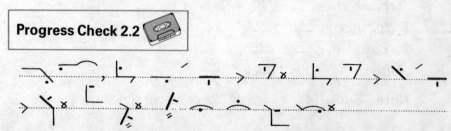

Short Forms

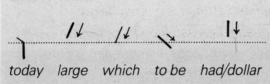

today   large   which   to be   had/dollar

Intersections

K —→ **company,** CH / **charge**
The intersection is written through the outline ⌣ **boom,**
⌣ **boom company,** *or the outline is written through the*
intersection ⌣ **, company boom.**

Progress Check 2.3

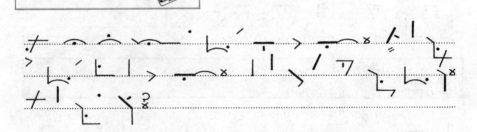

Vowel Review

*Before starting Unit 3 it is essential to have learned the vowels met
so far. When the theory of one unit has been understood and
mastered it is much easier to work with the new theory in the next
unit. Learning a skill involves laying a firm foundation and building
on it. The basic strokes and vowels are the essential foundation on
which to build shorthand skill. Drill the following outlines until
completely mastered.*

Heavy dot and dash vowels

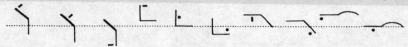

bought boat boot talk take teak cope keep calm came

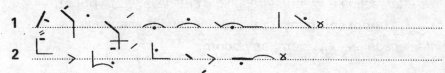

make   meek

Reading and Writing Practice

1

2

3

4

5

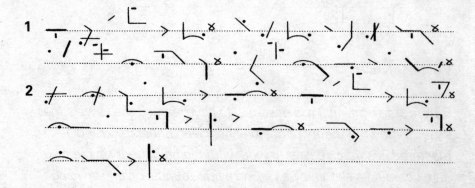

Dictation

1

2

Unit 3
Light dot vowels; strokes S and Z; circle S

Light Dot Vowels

1 *The next vowel sounds are light and are represented by a light dot:*

1st position   **a** *as in* **pack**
2nd position   **e** *as in* **peck**
3rd position   **i** *as in* **pick**

2 *Practise writing the following examples. Write each example several times, saying the word to yourself as you write; this is your own personal dictation and helps you to associate the sound with the outline. Remember to complete the joined strokes in one movement. Always write the stroke(s) first and then add the vowel(s).*

add   bag   catch   map   edge   jet   check   get   empty

pity   big   dig

Progress Check 3.1

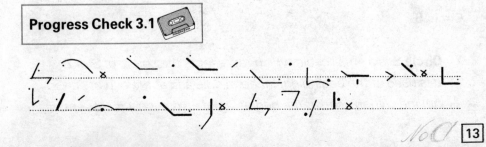

13

Strokes S and Z

The light sound of **S** *and the heavy sound of* **Z** *are represented by strokes and also by a circle. Where alternative forms for a sound are available the stroke is in all cases used for specific reasons, either vowel indication for ease of transcription or for ease of writing.*

1 **Stroke S** ⟩⌇ *is a thin downstroke.* **Stroke Z** ⟩⌇ *is a thick downstroke. The strokes are used as follows:*

   a   *When* **S/Z** *is the only consonant, to enable vowels to be placed:*

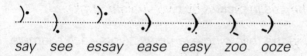

   say   see   essay   ease   easy   zoo   ooze

   b   *When* **Z** *begins a word, for ease of transcription:*

   zip   zoom

Progress Check 3.2

Circle S

1 **Circle S** *is a small circle which represents the sound of* **S** *or* **Z**. *It is used at the beginning, in the middle and at the end of an outline. When used at the beginning of an outline it represents*

the sound of **S** only. At the beginning of an outline the circle is read first; when at the end it is read last. It is written:

a *inside curves:*

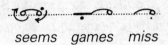

seems   games   miss

b *anti-clockwise to straight strokes:*

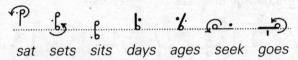

sat   sets   sits   days   ages   seek   goes

c *outside the angle formed by two straight strokes:*

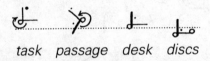

task   passage   desk   discs

Stroke S and Circle S

Now that you have met **circle S** *there are two other rules for* **stroke S**. *Write* **stroke S** *when:*

1 **S-vowel-S/Z begins a word:**

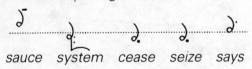

sauce   system   cease   seize   says

2 **Vowel-S/Z begins a word or S/Z-vowel ends a word, for vowel indication:**

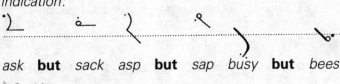

ask **but** sack   asp **but** sap   busy **but** bees

Vowel Indication

*The use of the **stroke S** or the **circle S** indicates the presence or absence of a vowel at the beginning and end of outlines. It is unnecessary therefore to place vowels in outlines using **stroke S**. It is essential at this stage however that you practise the placing of all other vowels.*

Progress Check 3.3

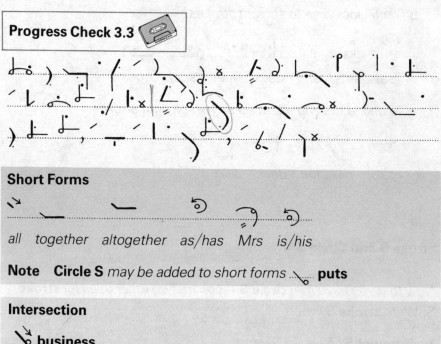

Short Forms

all   together   altogether   as/has   Mrs   is/his

Note   **Circle S** *may be added to short forms*   **puts**

Intersection

business

large business   company business

Phrases

Circle S *represents the following words:* **is, his, as, has, us**

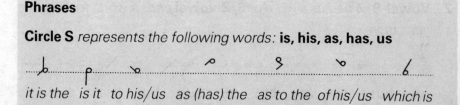

it is the   is it   to his/us   as (has) the   as to the   of his/us   which is

Vowel Review

Consolidate your knowledge of the vowels you have met. Drill each outline until you really do know it.

	ah	**a**	**e**
heavy dot			

pass calm ask   pay space say   see me easy

	aw	**o**	**oo**
heavy dash			

saw chalk   so chose dose   choose juice

	a	**e**	**i**
light dot			

catch adds   get beg edge   pity sit city

Reading and Writing Practice

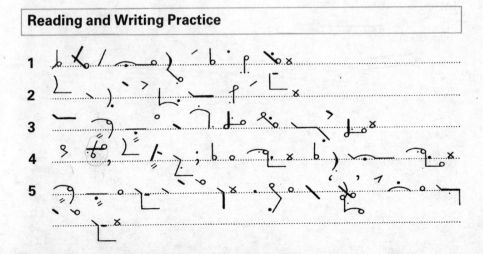

1
2
3
4
5

Dictation

1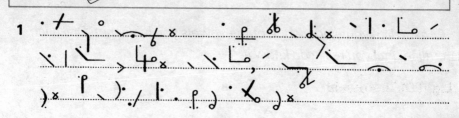

2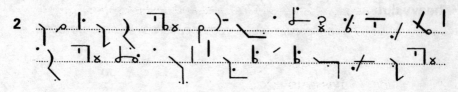

Unit 4
Light dash vowels; SES circle; ST and STER loops

Light Dash Vowels

There are three more vowels in the dots and dashes series, represented by a light dash:

1st position   **o** *as in* **job**
2nd position   **u** *as in* **up**
3rd position   **oo** *as in* **took**

Drill the examples which follow until you know them:

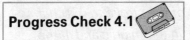

odd top job because us up suppose much such discuss book took

Progress Check 4.1

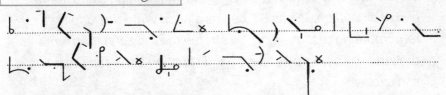

SES Circle, ST and STER Loops

In the writing of this circle and these loops the same rules apply as for the **circle S.**

SES Circle

1   **SES circle** *represents the sound of two* **S's** *(or* **S** *and* **Z***) and is written large, inside curves and anti-clockwise to straight strokes.*

19

*Always show the difference in size between the **circle S** and **SES** to enable you to read your notes without difficulty:*

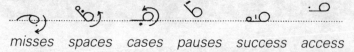

misses   spaces   cases   pauses   success   access

2 *A vowel, other than **e**, sounded between the two **S**'s is placed inside the circle:*

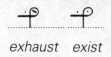

exhaust   exist

3 **Circle S** *may be added to the **SES circle**:*

diseases

ST Loop

1 **ST loop** *is shallow and half the length of the stroke to which it is attached. It is used at the beginning, in the middle and at the end of an outline. When **ST** begins a word write the loop first, remembering that it is long, so stretch the loop and then write the stroke. There must be a clear distinction between the loops and circles:*

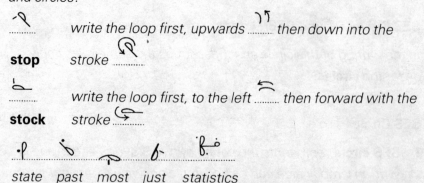

state   past   most   just   statistics

2 Circle S *may be added to the* **ST:**

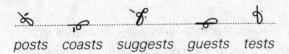

posts coasts suggests guests tests

3 ST loop *is not used when there is a vowel between the* **S** *and* **T,** *or when a vowel follows* **ST** *at the end of a word:*

cast cassette best beset bestow post upset

STER Loop

This is a large loop, to distinguish it from the **ST,** *and it is written two-thirds the length of the stroke to which it is attached. It is used in the middle and at the end of an outline.* **Circle S** *may be added:*

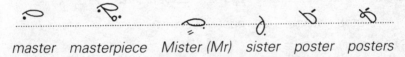

master masterpiece Mister (Mr) sister poster posters

Note *The difference in size of circles and loops is very important to enable you to read your notes and produce an accurate transcription:*

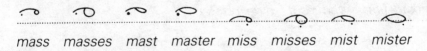

mass masses mast master miss misses mist mister

Progress Check 4.2

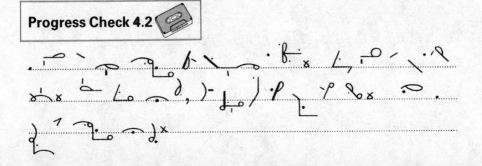

Vowel Review

This is the final review of the dot and dash vowels. Spend as much time as it takes to be able to write each outline without hesitancy. Do not proceed until you are confident writing all the 12 vowels.

heavy dot

ask past cast master pays cases states me seems keep

heavy dash

saw pause causes poses post goes most chooses stoop

light dot

at access statistics assist get best steps cities misses

light dash

stop stock up must success suggest took book

Short Forms

almost first who but owe/oh on

Phrases

1 **ST loop** *is used to represent the word* **first** *in addition to the short form:*

first-aid   at first

2 ST loop *in* **must** *is replaced by* **circle S,** *to give a good joining:*

must be

Note *A change of angle when* **tick the** *is added to* ...ι. **but,**
¹ **on,** ↙ **but the,** ↗ **on the.**

Reading and Writing Practice

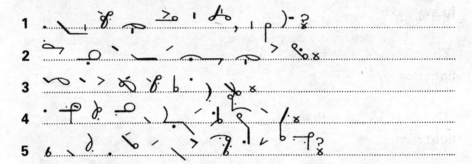

Dictation

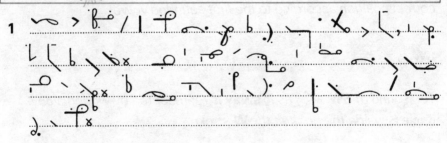

Unit 5
Strokes W, Y, SH, ZH, Th, TH; past tense; diphthongs

Strokes

W ⌐ as in **walk** ⌐

Y ℓ as in **yes** ℓ

SH (thin) ⫽ as in **show** ⋏

ZH (thick) ⫽ as in **beige** ⟩

Th (thin) ⟨ as in **oath** ⟨

TH (thick) ⟨ as in **them** ⟨

was	wages	week	wish	yes	use	shop	she	thick	they	them	these

Note It is the first downstroke or upstroke which is placed in the correct position according to the first sounded vowel.

SW

The sound of **SW** ⌐, as in **sway** is represented by writing a tiny **circle S** inside the hook of the **W** stroke:

⌐   write the first part of the circle upwards ⌐, close it by **sway** writing downwards ⌐ and then form the hook of the **W** ⌐.

sway	swim	switch	sweep

Past Tense

1 *The past tense for most verbs in our language is shown by writing* **T, D** *or* **ED** *at the end of the word. Sometimes the endings* **D** *and* **ED** *are pronounced as a* **T.** *Represent past tense outlines by writing a disjoined stroke* **T** *or* **D,** *whichever is pronounced, close to the root outline, including short forms:*

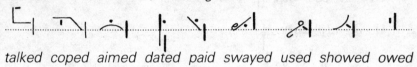

talked coped aimed dated paid swayed used showed owed

2 *Tick* **the** *may be added to the past tense stroke:*

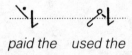

paid the   used the

Progress Check 5.1

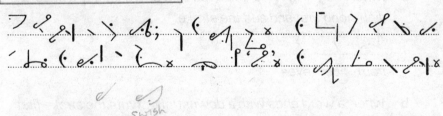

swish

Diphthongs and Triphones

1 *A* **diphthong** *is the technical name for the sound made when two vowels are pronounced together eg* **I** *as in* **my** *(to make the sound* **I** *two vowels are in fact sounded together). Note carefully the shape of each diphthong. Diphthongs are written in the first position and the third position; there are no second-place diphthongs.*

There are two first-place diphthongs:

I .... *as in* **my** ....

OI .... *as in* **joy** ....

There are two third-place diphthongs:

OW .... *as in* **out** ....

U .... *as in* **duty** ....

by/buy time side decide boy choice south mouth out

assume Tuesday occupy

2   *Diphthongs may be joined to strokes:*

a   *when* **I** *begins a word, followed by a downstroke; write the diphthong first and add the stroke:*

item   ice   eyes

b   *when a word ends with a downstroke; write the stroke first and add the diphthong:*

bow

c   *when a word ends with* **U** *the diphthong is attached, and can be turned to make a better joining:*

due   issue   queue/cue

3 *When another vowel is sounded immediately after a diphthong it is indicated by adding a tick, and this sign is called a* **triphone:**

bias   joyous

(More examples of triphones follow in later units.)

Progress Check 5.2

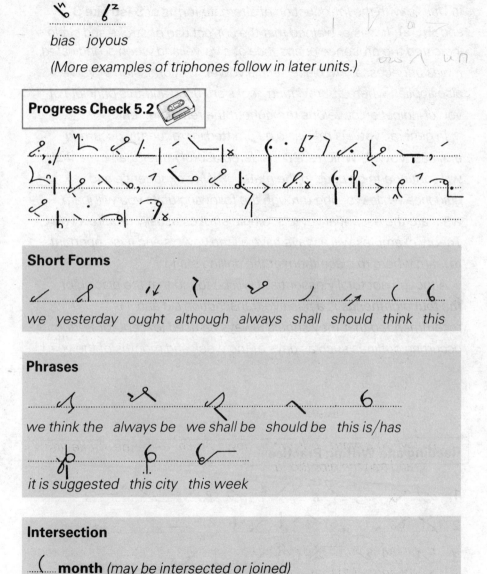

Short Forms

we   yesterday   ought   although   always   shall   should   think   this

Phrases

we think the   always be   we shall be   should be   this is/has

it is suggested   this city   this week

Intersection

month *(may be intersected or joined)*

some months   six months   this month

Vowel Indication

In Unit 3, with the introduction of alternate forms of **S (stroke S
and circle),** *it was explained that the correct use of stroke and circle
indicated the presence or absence of a vowel and when so indicated
it was unnecessary to place such a vowel. This omission of vowels
also applies where abbreviating hooks are used and this principle of
vowel indication develops throughout the remaining units.*

*In general, vowels may also be omitted in frequently occurring
outlines. Vowels which are considered useful rather than essential
will continue to be used in the material. With experience and
guidance while working through the following units you will learn
what are the essential vowels. Single strokes usually require a vowel.
Theory examples will always have all the vowels and it is important
to learn where to place them at the drilling stage.*

*Although not totally essential it will be found that the placing of
the four diphthongs is a positive transcription aid and it is
recommended that they should always be used (except for frequently
occurring outlines such as days of the week and months of the year).*

Reading and Writing Practice

Dictation

1 [shorthand outlines]

2 [shorthand outlines]

aei
ou oo
aw o ooh
ah ay ee

a e i o u

aeiou

Unit 6
Strokes F and V; F/V hook; dot ING; dash INGS

The sounds of **F** and **V** are represented by strokes and also by an abbreviating hook. The **F** and **V** hooks are used at the end of outlines, and are frequently used in the middle to give a briefer and faster outline.

F and V Strokes

1   **F** is a downward curved thin stroke ⤵ as in ⌇ **face.**

   V is a downward curved thick stroke ⤵ as in ⌇ **vague.**

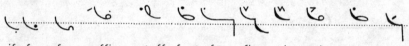

if fee few office staff fast fact five via voice vast vote

visit view save move shove cavity

2   Always use the stroke when the **F** or **V** is followed by a vowel or diphthong, to indicate the vowel or diphthong:

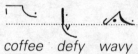

coffee   defy   wavy

Progress Check 6.1

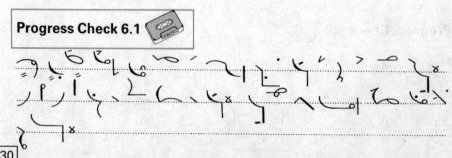

F/V Hook

1 *A brief way of representing* **F** *and* **V** *is a* **small** *hook written anti-clockwise at the end of straight strokes. There is no* **F/V hook** *to curves:*

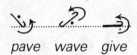

pave   wave   give

Write the hook when **F/V** *is the final sound, indicating no vowel follows:*

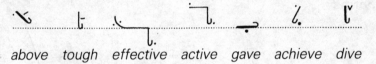

above   tough   effective   active   gave   achieve   dive

   a **Circle S** *may be added by writing a tiny circle inside the hook:*

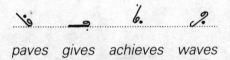

paves   gives   achieves   waves

2 *Write the hook medially, where the joining can be seen easily, giving a much briefer and very easy to read outline:*

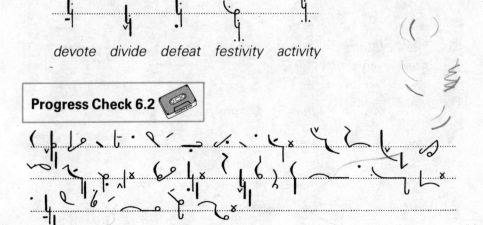

devote   divide   defeat   festivity   activity

Progress Check 6.2

Dot ING; Dash INGS

A dot at the end of an outline or short form represents the suffix **ING,** a dash represents **INGS.**

Write the dot or dash before placing any vowels; it is an essential part of an outline:

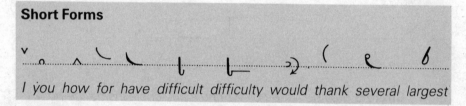

checking   takings   thinking   making   sayings   doing   buying

Short Forms

I   you   how   for   have   difficult   difficulty   would   thank   several   largest

Phrases

1   Only the first half of the short form ....., ... is used before **K, G** and **M:**

I came   I go   I am   I may

2   The short form .... **have** joins easily to form useful phrases:

I have   we have   they have   may have

3   **Have** is also represented by the hook:

you have   which have   who have   those who have

It is possible in a phrase to omit a word and still have an outline which can be transcribed without any problem:

ought to have

4 The hook also represents the words **of** and **off**:

copy of   set of   state of   out of   get off   set off   to take off

5 The outline ⌐ **much** forms useful phrases:

so much   too much   how much   as much as

Intersection

form

this form   take form   several forms   top form   some form

Reading and Writing Practice

1

2

3

4

5

Dictation

Memo

To: Fay Smith   **From: Joseph James**
Subject: Staffing   **Date: Today's**

Unit 7
Stroke R

The sound of **R** is represented by two strokes, and also by an abbreviating hook which is introduced in the next unit. Once again you will find that the strokes are used mainly to indicate the presence or absence of a vowel, or for easier writing.

There are two forms of **stroke R,** the upward ......✐... and the downward ...✐.....

Upward R

Upward R is a straight, light upstroke .../..... (check the difference in angle between this stroke and downward **CH** ../......).

1 Upward R ..../.....is used:

a when **R** begins a word, indicating there is no previous vowel:

rate read ready receive rest right/write road reach

b in the middle of an outline. When there is an **R** in the spelling it is represented in the shorthand outline even though at times it is hardly pronounced. This assists you to read and readily transcribe the outlines:

work word purpose Thursday party marked service exercise

Note   Diphthong ...., the same as a vowel, may be placed inside the **SES circle,** as in ...✐..... **exercise.**

35

c *when* **R-vowel** *ends a word, indicating the presence of a final vowel:*

borrow   diary   memory   carry   sorry   thorough   story   factory

This final **upward R** *indicates the presence of a final vowel and therefore there is no need to insert the vowel when taking dictation.*

Progress Check 7.1

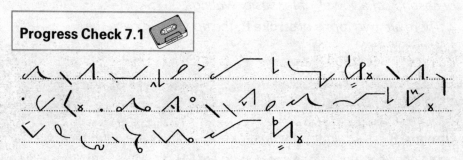

Downward R

Write the stroke as follows:

1 *When* **vowel-R** *begins a word, indicating the presence of a vowel:*

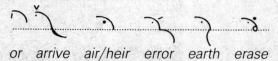

or   arrive   air/heir   error   earth   erase

Once you have practised these outlines, and mastered them, there is generally no need to place the first vowel. Always write a vowel if you feel it to be essential for accurate transcription.

2 *Before* **M**, *to make an easier joining making a sharper angle:*

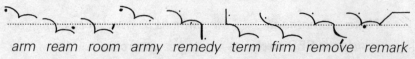

arm   ream   room   army   remedy   term   firm   remove   remark

3 When **R** ends a word, indicating that there is no final vowel; **downward R** is retained in derivatives:

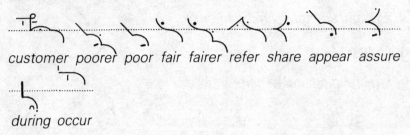

customer poorer poor fair fairer refer share appear assure

during occur

4 When immediately followed by **circle S** or **SES** or **ST loop**, indicating there is no vowel between the **R** and the **circle S**:

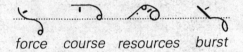

force   course   resources   burst

Note   By using the correct stroke **R**, vowels are indicated and therefore should be omitted from outlines:

care   carry   sure   sherry   bar   borrow   urge   arch

Progress Check 7.2

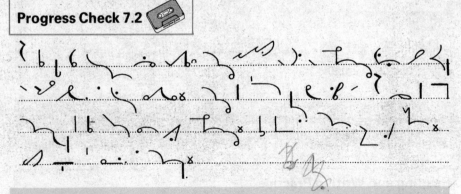

Short Forms

are   hour/our   satisfactory   your   tomorrow   year   with

Intersections

......)....arrange, arranged, arrangement

......)....arranging

....../....require, required, requirement

we have arranged   make arrangements   they may arrange

they require   you may be required   your requirements

Phrases

1 we are   they are   they were   of your   to your   to our

I am sorry   with us

2 Only the first half of the short form .... , ... is used before **upward R:**

I wrote   I read   I received

Reading and Writing Practice

1

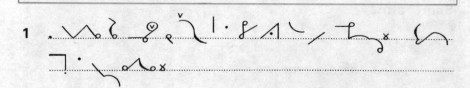

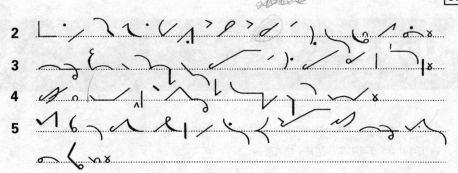

2

3

4

5

 Dictation

1 Memo

To: All Staff   From: Factory Fire Officer
Subject: Safety

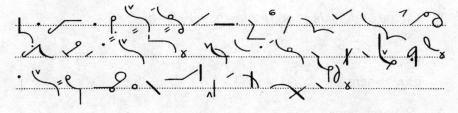

2 Memo

To: Factory Fire Officer   From: Chief Fire Officer
Subject: First-aid Boxes

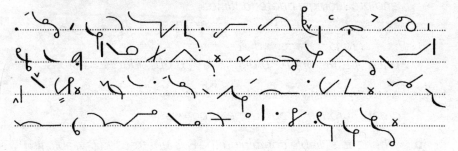

Unit 8
R hook

The **R hook** *is the other way to represent the sound of* **R.** *Always write it as a small, tight hook.*

The R Hook to straight strokes

1   *The hook is written on the left side (clockwise) of downstrokes:*

price   try

2   *On the underside of horizontals (clockwise):*

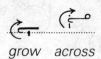

grow   across

3   *Write the hook:*

a   *at the beginning or in the middle of an outline when a consonant and* **R** *are sounded together with no vowel between, (consonantally) indicating the absence of a vowel and producing a briefer outline:*

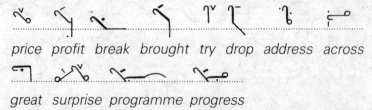

price   profit   break   brought   try   drop   address   across

great   surprise   programme   progress

b   *when the syllable containing the* **R** *is unstressed (syllabically). (In words of more than one syllable each syllable is either*

40

stressed or unstressed, according to the correct pronunciation; most dictionaries show which syllables are stressed; it is enough that you appreciate the reason for the rule and simply write the correct outline through adequate practice.)

paper figure major remember maker December

perform correct

Note When the syllable containing **R** is unstressed the abbreviating **R hook** is used, and when the syllable is stressed the **stroke R** is written. The correct application of these rules produces accurate notes capable of rapid, accurate transcription.

Progress Check 8.1

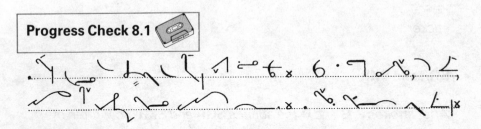

Circle S and R Hook

1   For words beginning with the sound **SPR-, STR-** or **SKR-** write a complete circle in the same direction as **hook R**: ＼, ⌇ and ⌒.

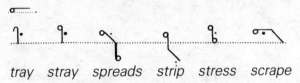

tray   stray   spreads   strip   stress   scrape

2 *Both* **circle S** *and the hook are shown when combined in the middle of an outline. Write a tiny circle and then form the hook by writing upwards:*

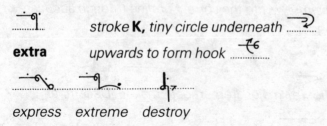

stroke **K,** *tiny circle underneath*

extra *upwards to form hook*

express   extreme   destroy

ST Loop and R Hook

ST loop *is incorporated by writing the complete loop first (from right to left), to be placed on the* **R hook** *side, and then writing the stroke:*

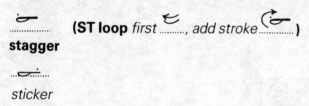

stagger **(ST loop** *first* ...., *add stroke* ....)

sticker

SGR and SKR

After strokes **P, B** *and* **D** *the sounds* **SGR** *and* **SKR** *are written by completing the downstroke and adding the* **circle S:**

dis

and after completing the **circle S** *write the horizontal stroke on top of the circle:*

disagree

disgrace   disagree   describe   prescribe   subscribe

Progress Check 8.2

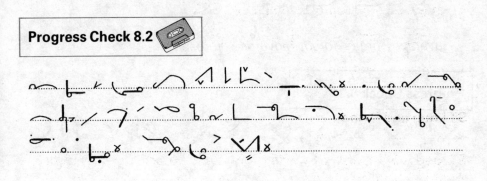

The R Hook to curved strokes

R hook *to curved strokes follows the same rules as* **R hook** *to straight strokes. A much briefer and more distinctive outline is produced.*

1   *The hook is small and written at the beginning of curved strokes, writing the hook first and then writing the stroke:*

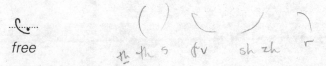

free

2   *Write the hook at the beginning and inside the curve when a consonant and* **R** *are sounded together with no vowel between (consonantally):*

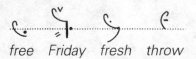

free   Friday   fresh   throw

3 *Use the hook within an unstressed syllable (syllabically):*

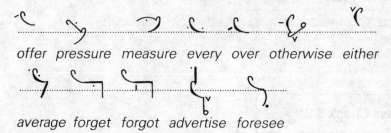

offer   pressure   measure   every   over   otherwise   either

average forget forgot advertise foresee

Progress Check 8.3

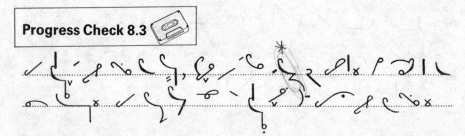

Circle S

The circle may be added by writing a tiny circle first and wrapping the small hook around it in outlines where the hooked syllable is unstressed:

sever   summer   suffer   safer

Reversed FR, VR, ThR and THR

Hooked strokes **FR** ⌣ , **VR** ⌣ , **ThR** ⌣ *and* **THR** ⌣
are always reversed ⟩⟩⟩⟩⟩ *after horizontal and upstrokes
to make an easier joining:*

wafer   cover   discover   recover   recovery   rather   gather   weather

Progress Check 8.4

(shorthand outlines)

Short Forms

(shorthand outlines)

dear   from   before   more   their/there   commercial/commercially

(shorthand outlines)

very   larger

Intersection

(shorthand outline) **corporation**

Phrases

1

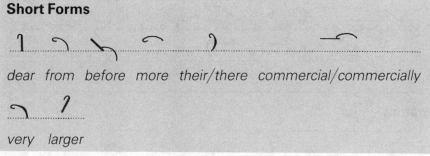

Dear Sir   very much   there is   there are   there may be   I gather

Yours faithfully   of course   free of charge   very satisfactory

2   Abbreviated diphthong ⌄ , ＼ , before a hooked stroke:

I trust   I agree

Reading and Writing Practice

1

2

3

4

5

Dictation

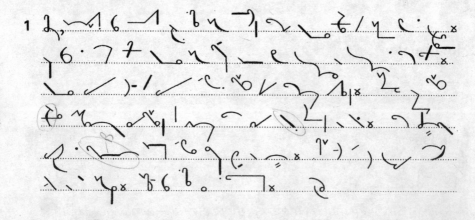

1

2

Unit 9
Strokes N, NG; N hook

There are two ways of representing the sound **N**, the **stroke N** and the **hook N**. Once again it will be found that the indication of vowels is the main reason for using one instead of the other. The hook is only used when **N** is the last sound in a word (suffixes may be added).

Stroke N

1 **Stroke N** is thin and shallow, a scooped-out curve:

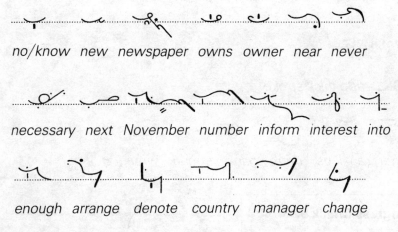

no/know new newspaper owns owner near never

necessary next November number inform interest into

enough arrange denote country manager change

2 Always use the stroke:

   a when **N-vowel** ends a word, to indicate a final vowel:

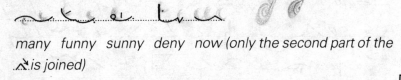

many funny sunny deny now (only the second part of the
 is joined)

48

b *for the light sound **NS,** to distinguish from the heavier sound of **NZ** which is represented by the hook:* (coming after a curved stroke)

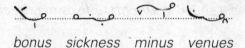

announce   occurrence   reference   insurance

c *when a vowel or diphthong occurs between **N** and **S/Z,** to enable the vowel to be placed as a transcription aid:*

bonus   sickness   minus   venues

d *after a medial circle for a much easier joining:*

design   resign   basin   dozen

Stroke NG

NG  *is a thick stroke:*

anger   anxious   drink   bank   strong   wrong

Progress Check 9.1

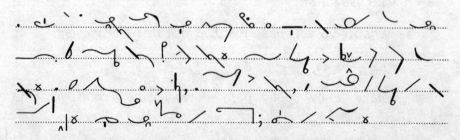

Hook N

Hook N *is written at the end of a stroke, inside curves* ⌣ **fine,** *and on the non-**circle S** side (clockwise) to straight strokes,* ⌐ **town.**

Remember that the **F/V hook** *is written anti-clockwise to straight strokes* ╞ **tough,** *and is not applied to curves.*

This abbreviating hook is used when there is no vowel to be placed and indicates the absence of any vowel, which aids transcription. Use the hook:

1 When **N** is the final sound in a word:

often even mine man woman machine open can been

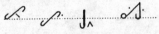

one win down certain

2 For the sound of **NS** or **NZ**, where **circle S** is added to **hook N** to straight strokes by closing the hook:

bounce tins wines returns joins expense

3 For the sound of **NZ** only where the **circle S** is reduced in size and written inside the hook to curves: *(curved stroke)*

fines means examines

Note **SES circle, ST** *and* **STER loops** *are added to straight strokes hooked for* **N** *by writing the circle or loop on the* **hook N** *side and incorporating the hook:*

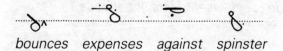

bounces   expenses   against   spinster

Note **Hook R** *and* **hook N** *are written on the same side of straight strokes:*

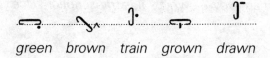

green   brown   train   grown   drawn

Progress Check 9.2

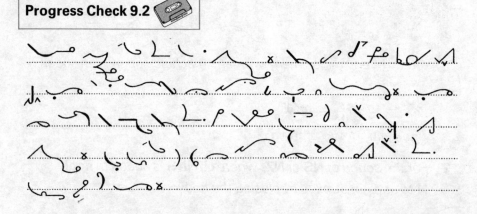

Short Forms

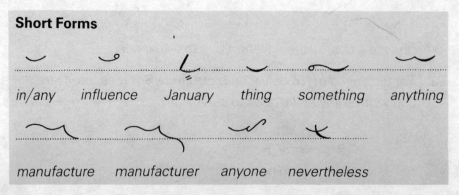

in/any   influence   January   thing   something   anything

manufacture   manufacturer   anyone   nevertheless

notwithstanding   *responsible/responsibility*

Intersections

enquire, enquiry, inquire, inquiry:

your enquiry/inquiry   several enquiries/inquiries   we shall enquire

Phrases

The **N hook** *is used to represent the words* **been, than** *and* **own:**

I have been   I had been   already been   there has been   it has been

better than   more than   rather than   bigger than   larger than

your own   our own   their own

The word **once** *is abbreviated in phrases:*

at once   once again

The word **next** *is abbreviated in phrases:*

next few days   next month   next week

Note *In compound words derived from root words using **hook N** the hook is retained and the following part of the outline is joined or disjoined. This rule has very few applications and is given for information only. The examples are not used in any of the practice material:*

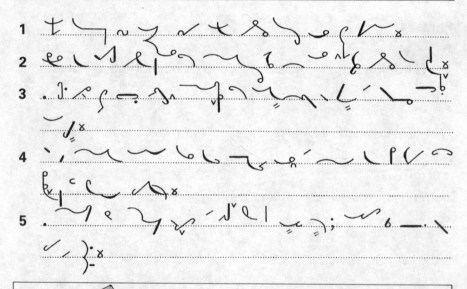

manpower   earthenware   brainstorm

Reading and Writing Practice

1

2

3

4

5

Dictation 🗂

---

1 Letter to the Manager, Evening News

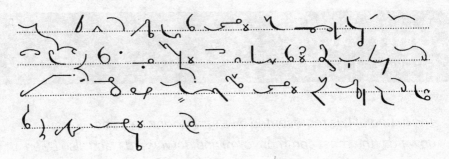

2 Memo

To: All Staff　　　**From: Manager**
Subject: Overtime　**Date: Today's**

short form

shor

short

Unit 10
Stroke L; L hook

The sound of **L** is represented by a stroke which can be written
upwards (the most common form) and downwards, and also by an
abbreviating hook. Once again the use of the stroke and the hook
is governed mainly by the vowels involved in an outline. The hook
is used consonantally when there is no vowel between the stroke
and the hook or syllabically, when the syllable is unstressed.

Upward Stroke L

1 **Upward stroke L** is thin and curved and is written:

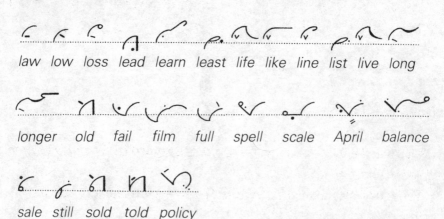

law   low   loss   lead   learn   least   life   like   line   list   live   long

longer   old   fail   film   full   spell   scale   April   balance

sale   still   sold   told   policy

a When **OI** precedes **L** at the beginning of a word, the diphthong
OI is joined. Write the diphthong first:

oil   oiled   oiling

b *When a diphthong occurs in an unstressed syllable, the stroke is written to place the diphthong:*

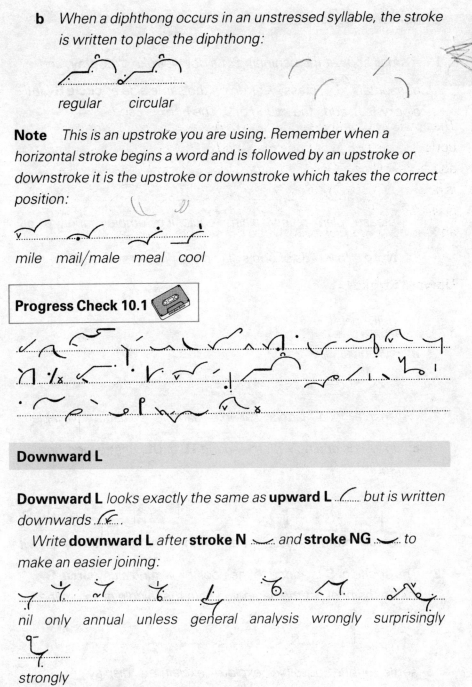

regular   circular

Note *This is an upstroke you are using. Remember when a horizontal stroke begins a word and is followed by an upstroke or downstroke it is the upstroke or downstroke which takes the correct position:*

mile   mail/male   meal   cool

Progress Check 10.1

Downward L

Downward L *looks exactly the same as* **upward L** *but is written downwards.*

Write **downward L** *after* **stroke N** *and* **stroke NG** *to make an easier joining:*

nil   only   annual   unless   general   analysis   wrongly   surprisingly

strongly

L Hook to straight strokes

1 *A small hook at the beginning of a downstroke,* 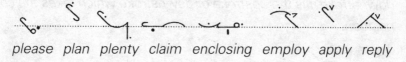 *play, and horizontals,* **class,** *written on the same side as* **circle S** *(anti-clockwise), adds the sound of* **L.** *The hook is used:*

a *consonantally, a consonant and* **L** *with no vowel between:*

please plan plenty claim enclosing employ apply reply

Note *In words of one syllable the hook is not used:*

pull   pale

b *syllabically:*

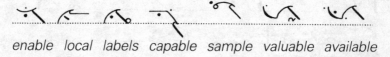

enable local labels capable sample valuable available

c *in words ending with the sound* **TL** *or* **DL,** *unstressed, however spelt:*

battle metal middle model mental instrumental rental vital

2 *The sound of* **S** *is added to the hook by writing a tiny* **circle S** *inside the hook, at the beginning or in the middle of an outline:*

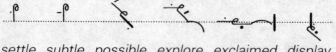

settle subtle possible explore exclaimed display

*(When writing **explore** ensure the combined **S** and **L** does not look just like a **circle S** by 'flicking' back along the horizontal stroke*

.)

a   *When the hook is used in a root outline it is retained in derivatives:*

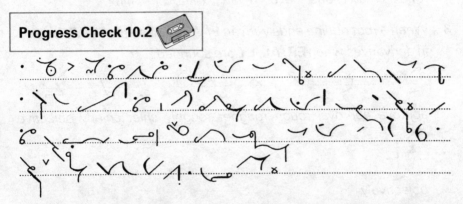

possibility

Progress Check 10.2

L Hook to curved strokes

1   *A large hook at the beginning of a curved stroke adds the sound of **L**. It is used consonantally and syllabically at the beginning and in the middle of an outline:*

fly   flow   travel   traveller   arrival   initial   partial   specialist

a   **Circle S** *may be added by writing a tiny circle inside the hook:*

civil

b *A final vowel may be added to the hooked curve; this is an essential vowel and must always be written:*

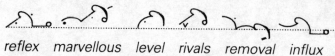

finally   financially   officially   originally   specially

2 *Hooked curved strokes* **FL** ⌒ *and* **VL** ⌒ *are always reversed when immediately following an upstroke or a horizontal:*

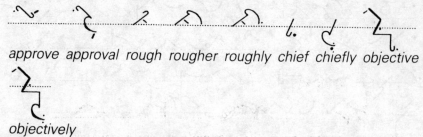

reflex   marvellous   level   rivals   removal   influx

3 *When a root outline ends with an* **F/V hook** *use the* **FL/VL hook** *in derivatives when* **ER, AL, LY** *are sounded:*

approve   approval   rough   rougher   roughly   chief   chiefly   objective

objectively

Note *When there is an unstressed syllable* **consonant-vowel-L,** *use the hook and omit the vowel. There are very few examples of this rule.*

fulfil   philosophy

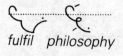

Progress Check 10.3

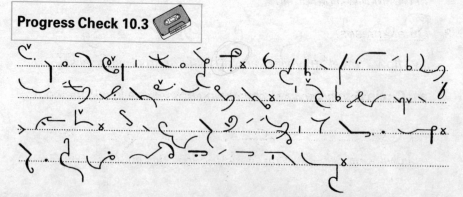

Short Forms

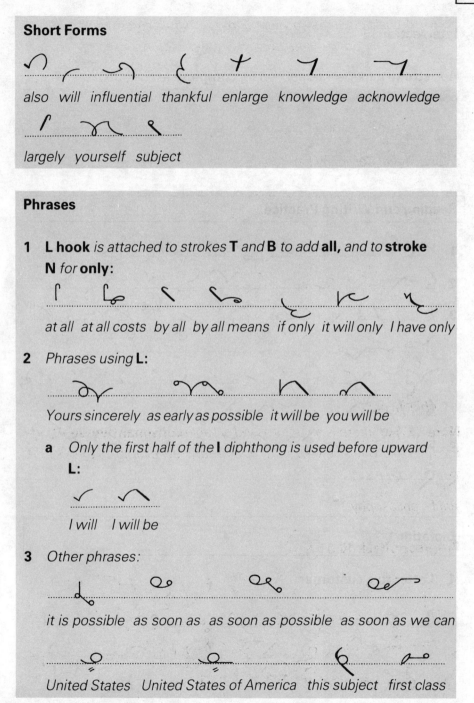

also   will   influential   thankful   enlarge   knowledge   acknowledge

largely   yourself   subject

Phrases

1   L hook *is attached to strokes* **T** *and* **B** *to add* **all,** *and to* **stroke N** *for* **only:**

at all   at all costs   by all   by all means   if only   it will only   I have only

2 *Phrases using* **L:**

Yours sincerely   as early as possible   it will be   you will be

a *Only the first half of the* **I** *diphthong is used before upward* **L:**

I will   I will be

3 *Other phrases:*

it is possible   as soon as   as soon as possible   as soon as we can

United States   United States of America   this subject   first class

Intersection

Add **stroke L** *to the intersection for* **company** *to give*
company limited.

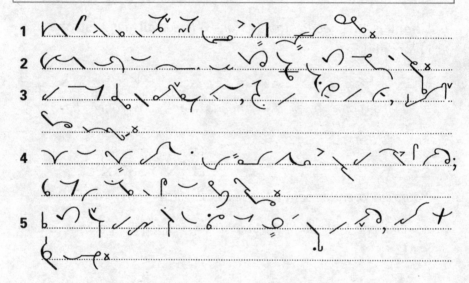

World Travel Company Limited

Reading and Writing Practice

1
2
3
4
5

Dictation

1 Letter to a customer

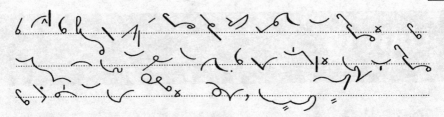

2 Letter to a friend

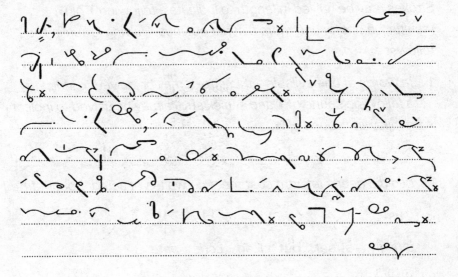

Unit 11
Halving; stroke H and tick H

Half Length Strokes

Strokes may be halved in length to indicate a following **T** *or* **D,**
resulting in briefer and more distinct outlines. Halving is applied as
follows:

1 *In words of one syllable a thin stroke may be halved to indicate*
  a following sound of **T** *and a thick stroke may be halved to indicate*
  a following sound of **D:**

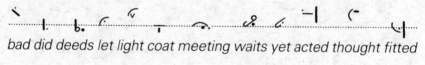

bad did deeds let light coat meeting waits yet acted thought fitted

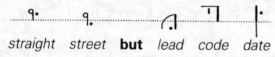

straight   street   **but**   lead   code   date

2 *Strokes with a finally attached diphthong or final hook may be*
  halved for **T** *or* **D,** *producing outlines which are easy to transcribe:*

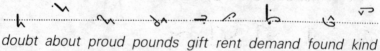

doubt   about   proud   pounds   gift   rent   demand   found   kind

3 *Strokes in words of more than one syllable may be halved for*
  T *or* **D:**

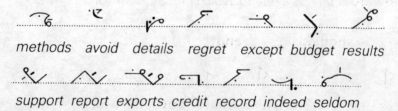

methods   avoid   details   regret   except   budget   results

support   report   exports   credit   record   indeed   seldom

Non-use of halving

Halving is not used when:

1 *A half-length stroke with a joined diphthong is followed by the sound of* **S,** *as it is not possible to add* **circle S** *to a diphthong:*

doubts

2 *The halving would not clearly show:*

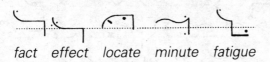

fact   effect   locate   minute   fatigue

3 *A vowel follows final stroke* **T** *or* **D.** *The writing of the stroke indicates a following vowel:*

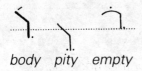

body   pity   empty

4 *A vowel comes between* **L-D, R-D,** *for vowel indication:*

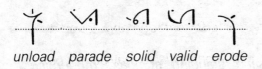

unload   parade   solid   valid   erode

5 **Upward R** *stands alone to avoid confusion with short forms*

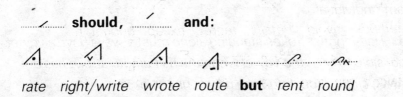

should,   and:

rate   right/write   wrote   route   **but**   rent   round

Disjoined Strokes

Strokes of unequal length must not be joined unless there is an angle at the joining. These strokes are disjoined for legibility:

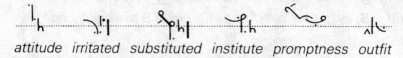

attitude irritated substituted institute promptness outfit

Progress Check 11.1

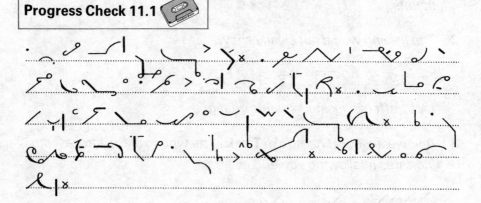

Strokes MD and ND

Strokes M *and* **N** *are halved and thickened to indicate the following sound of* **D:**

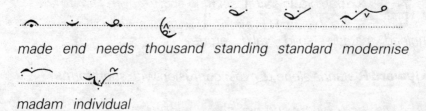

made end needs thousand standing standard modernise

madam individual

Note *Half-length strokes standing alone must always have a vowel. It is possible to omit the vowel when the half-length stroke has a* **dot -ING,** *circle, loop, hook or a past-tense stroke:*

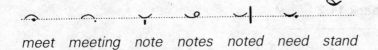

meet meeting note notes noted need stand

Stroke and Tick H

1 **Stroke H** 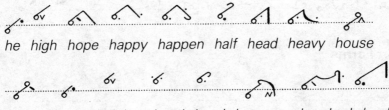 is written upwards:

he high hope happy happen half head heavy house

whose heat height ahead hand however hundred hard

a *Medial* **stroke H** *is written by writing the circle as if it was a* **circle S,** *that is anti-clockwise, and then writing the remainder of the stroke upwards:*

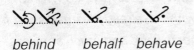

behind behalf behave

Note H *in the middle of a word following* **circle S** *is omitted:* mishap, household.

2 **Tick H** *is written downwards, slanting sharply from right to left* , *and is used when* **H** *is sounded before* **strokes M, L** *and* **downward R:**

him himself whom home help hold her herself hear/here

health whole

Progress Check 11.2

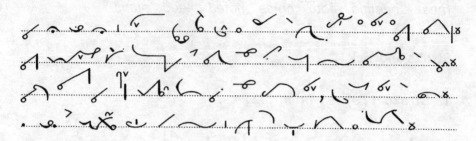

Short Forms

immediate immediately could that able to cannot particular

particularly accord/according/according to accordingly

Note The new short form ⟨⟨ **that** must always be written
precisely to avoid any confusion with the already learned short form
с with. One is heavy and the other is light, and much smaller.
Practise drilling them together and show the marked difference
between the two:

с ⟨ с ⟨ с

with that with that with

Phrases

Halving is used extensively in phrasing:

1 It A stroke may be halved to indicate **it:**

if it is in which it is I think it is necessary if it is possible

2 **Would**   In addition to the short form ...⊃., half-length ...⟋. is used when a better joining is obtained:

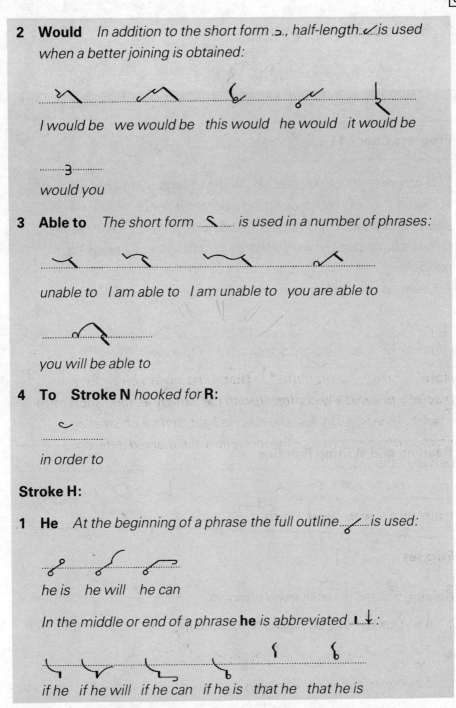

I would be   we would be   this would   he would   it would be

would you

3 **Able to**   The short form ..⊂.. is used in a number of phrases:

unable to   I am able to   I am unable to   you are able to

you will be able to

4 **To**   **Stroke N** hooked for **R**:

in order to

Stroke H:

1 **He**   At the beginning of a phrase the full outline...⟋. is used:

he is   he will   he can

In the middle or end of a phrase **he** is abbreviated .⎍.↓.:

if he   if he will   if he can   if he is   that he   that he is

2 Hope *The **H** is omitted:*

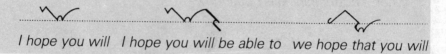

I hope you will   I hope you will be able to   we hope that you will

---

Progress Check 11.3

This progress check will help you with the large number of phrases in this unit. When you understand a phrasing principle you will be able to apply it readily. Phrases are not lists of words to be learned by heart but groups of words within a framework of a phrasing principle.

Further phrasing principles involving halving appear in Unit 12.

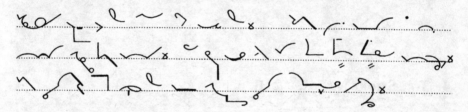

Reading and Writing Practice

1

2

3

4

5

Dictation

1 Letter to Mr N Holmes

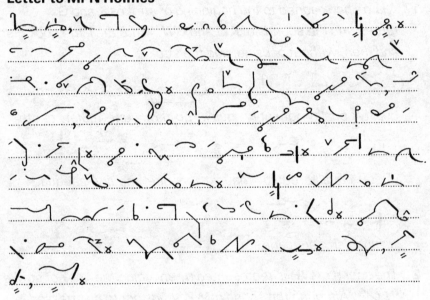

2 Memo

To: Sales Manager   From: Personnel Manager
Subject: Peter Adamson, Sales Staff

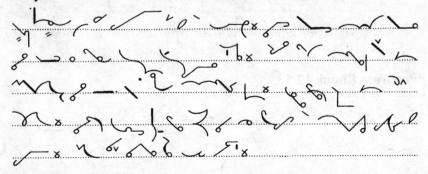

Unit 12
Strokes KW, GW, WH; Diphones

Strokes KW, GW and WH

1   A large hook added to the beginning of strokes **K** and **G** represents the sounds of **KW** and **GW.** Write the large hook first and then, without pausing, add the stroke:

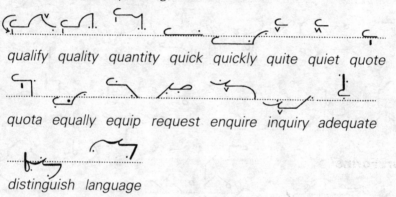

qualify quality quantity quick quickly quite quiet quote

quota equally equip request enquire inquiry adequate

distinguish language

2   The sound of **WH** is represented by enlarging the hook of stroke **W**  Although the sound of **WH** tends not to be stressed in our use of the language its representation in outlines results in distinctive outlines:

what whatever when whenever where whether why while white

Progress Check 12.1

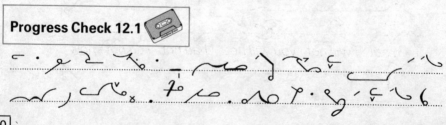

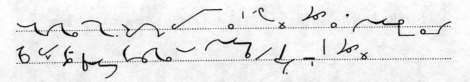

Diphones

*When two vowel sounds follow each other they are represented by the sign.ɪ., called a **diphone,** and it is written in the position of the first of the two vowel sounds. There are many examples of the use of diphones but most outlines can be transcribed without placing the diphone. The examples are limited to those outlines where the placement of the diphone is considered essential. The omission of these diphones would make transcription very difficult.*

| area | radio | create | idea | lowest | **but** | earlier (safely omitted) |

Short Forms

| trade/toward | gentleman | gentlemen |

Phrases

*Phrases involving **halving** were introduced in Unit 11. The following additional words are represented by use of halving:*

1 Not

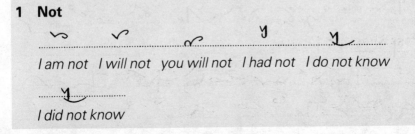

| I am not | I will not | you will not | I had not | I do not know |

| I did not know |

Stroke N *is halved to represent* **not** *in the following phrases:*

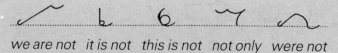

we are not   it is not   this is not   not only   were not

2 Time, out, state/statement

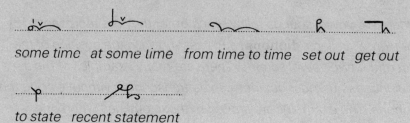

some time   at some time   from time to time   set out   get out

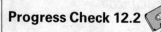

to state   recent statement

Progress Check 12.2

Reading and Writing Practice

1

2

3

4

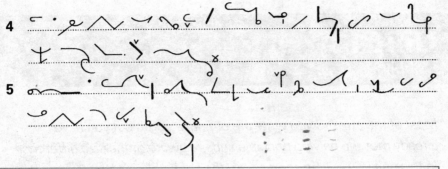

5

Dictation

1 Memo to: Manufacturing Manager   From: General Manager
Subject: Quality Checks   Date: Today's

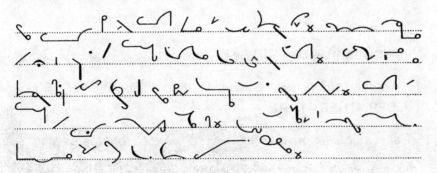

2 Letter to Miss Jean Cook from the Chief Personnel Officer

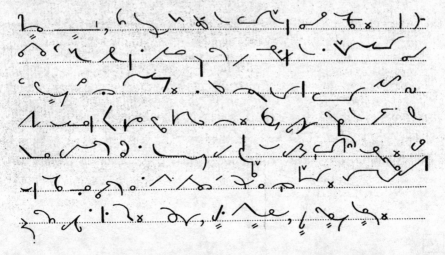

Unit 13
Doubling

Most of the strokes you write are ordinary length but you have already met the halving principle and are aware of the size difference. In this unit you will be shown how to use double-length strokes. The presence and the value of half-length and double-length strokes can only be appreciated if you are consistent in your writing of the ordinary strokes. When you transcribe your notes it must be perfectly clear to you that each stroke is either ordinary, half or double length.

Double-length curved strokes

1 A curved stroke is doubled in length for the addition of **-TER, -DER, -THER, -TURE**.

a Double-length downstrokes are written through the line:

after   afternoon   father   voter   ordered   Easter   future

b Upstrokes and horizontals are positioned according to the first sounded vowel:

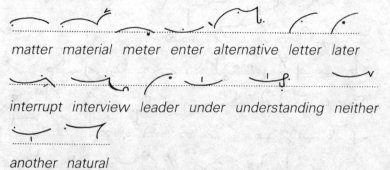

matter   material   meter   enter   alternative   letter   later

interrupt   interview   leader   under   understanding   neither

another   natural

c *A curved stroke may be doubled in the middle or at the end of an outline:*

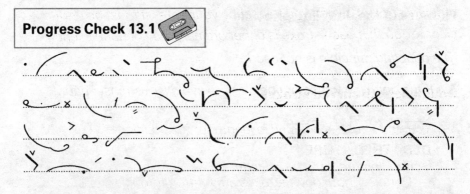

misunderstand builder folder calculator signature furniture

d *A curved stroke may be doubled when there is an initial or final circle or hook:*

centre softer flatter features reminder calendar

Progress Check 13.1

Double-length straight strokes

Double-length straight strokes on their own could present a problem when transcribing. For example .... Is it **pop,** *with two stroke* **Ps,** *or is it* **potter,** *with one stroke* **P** *doubled? In fact it is* **pop,** *as you will appreciate from the rules which follow:*

1 *A straight stroke is doubled in length for the addition of* **-TER, -DER, -THER, -TURE:**

    a *when following another stroke:*

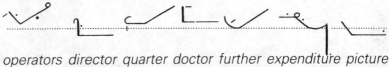

operators director quarter doctor further expenditure picture

b *when it has a final hook:*

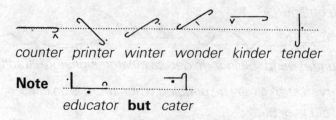

counter printer winter wonder kinder tender

Note educator **but** cater

Non-use of the doubling principle

The doubling principle is not used:

1 *If the doubling would not be clear, to avoid a mistranscription:*

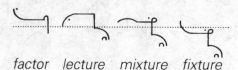

factor lecture mixture fixture

2 *When there is a final vowel:*

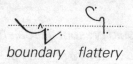

boundary flattery

3 *The doubling principle is not used in the middle of an outline to straight strokes:*

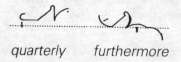

quarterly furthermore

Progress Check 13.2

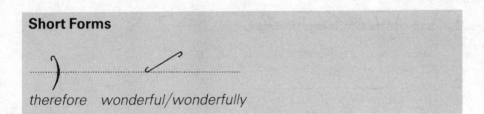

Short Forms

therefore   wonderful/wonderfully

Phrases

1 *A stroke may be doubled in phrases for the addition of* **their/there, other, order:**

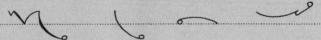

I know there is   I think there is   in there/their   in their opinion

I believe there is   if there is   some other   in other ways

2   Stroke N *hooked for* **R** *is doubled for the addition of* **order:**

in order that

3 *The word* **fact** *is represented by a half-length stroke* **K,** *joined or written close.*

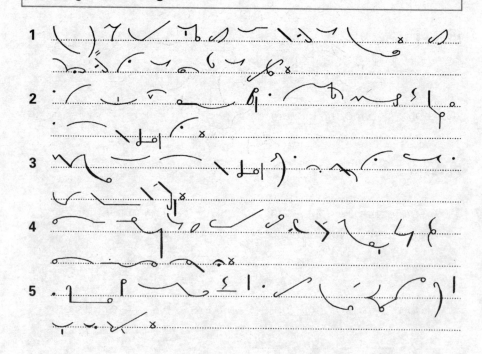

in fact   as a matter of fact   of the fact that   to the fact that

---

Reading and Writing Practice

Dictation

1 Letter to Sarah James about an interview

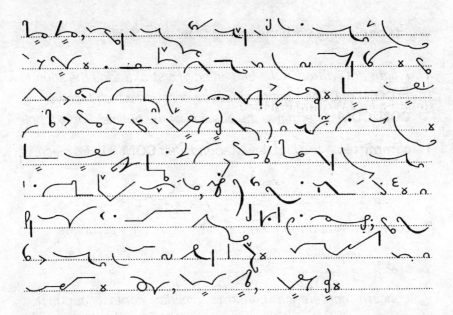

2 Interviews

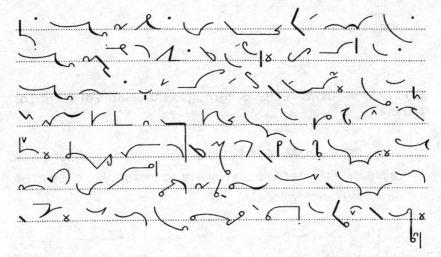

Unit 14

Words beginning with the sound CON and COM

1   *A light dot written at the beginning of a stroke adds the sound of* **CON-** *or* **COM-,** *but the first vowel sound which follows* **CON/COM** *determines the position of the outline. For example:*

committee—*the first vowel sound after* **COM** *is* **i,** *3rd place,* .

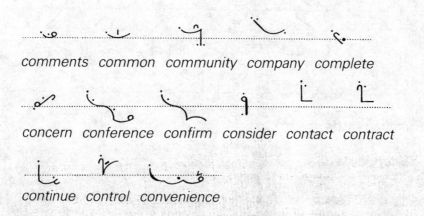

comments   common   community   company   complete

concern   conference   confirm   consider   contact   contract

continue   control   convenience

CON-/COM-/CUM-/COG- occurring in the middle of a word or phrase

1   *When* **CON-/COM-/CUM-/COG-** *occur in the middle of a word or phrase indicate the sound by writing two strokes close to each other and omitting the dot:*

discontinue   uncommon   recommend   circumstances

recognise incompetent   I am confident will continue

I will consider very common

Progress Check 14.1

Negative Words

The importance of the meaning of a negative word is highlighted by adding an additional stroke which is not needed phonetically but which ensures perfect transcription. To describe something as **legal** ......, *is simple enough; the description* **illegal** *makes a great difference in meaning and yet should only involve an additional vowel* ...... *. The omission of the vowel would give a meaning opposite to that intended and therefore it is safer to write negative words as follows:*

1 *Words which have the prefix* **IL-, IM-, IN-, UN-** *are written by repeating the* **L, M** *or* **N:**

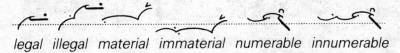

legal illegal material immaterial numerable innumerable

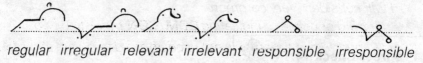

necessary   unnecessary

2   Words which have the prefix **IR-** are written with a **downward R** immediately before the **upward R**:

regular   irregular   relevant   irrelevant   responsible   irresponsible

3   Other negative words are written as they are sounded:

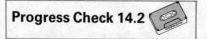

patient   impatient   reliable   unreliable   fortunately   unfortunately

---

Progress Check 14.2

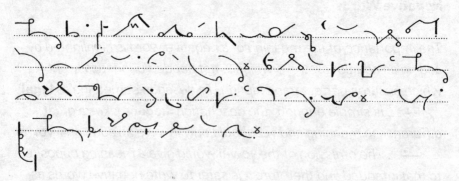

Short Forms

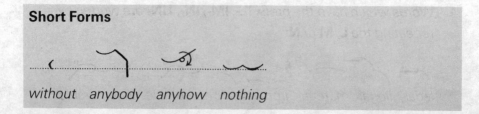

without   anybody   anyhow   nothing

Phrases

income tax   in control   by contrast   would be considered

This phrasing principle of indicating **COM**/**CON** by writing two
strokes/signs close together is not used after a downward short form
or the short forms .... **the** *or* .... **a:**

on committees   to commit   to complete   all concerned

the committee   a committee

Reading and Writing Practice

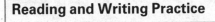

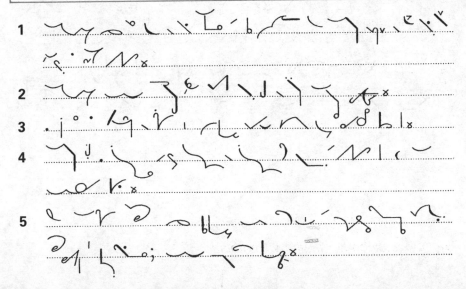

Dictation

1 Letter to the Manager, Ace Advertising Limited

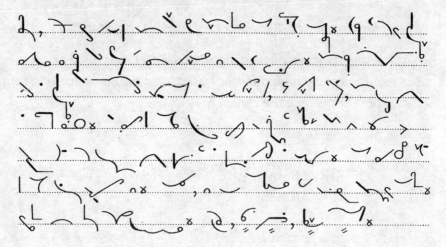

2 Memo to: All Staff   Subject: Annual Holiday

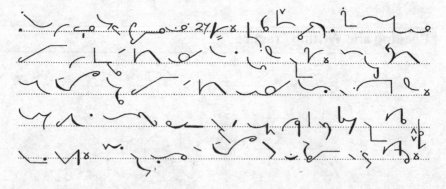

Unit 15
SHUN

*The sound **SHUN** is spelt in various ways but in Pitman Shorthand only two main methods of representing this sound are used, a large and a small hook.*

SHUN hook inside curves

1 *The large **SHUN hook** may be written in the middle or at the end of an outline. **Circle S** may be added:*

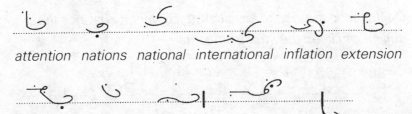

attention nations national international inflation extension

explanation fashion mentioned cancellation division

2 *A third-place dot vowel is written inside the hook, other third-place vowel signs outside:*

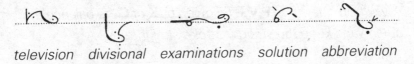

television divisional examinations solution abbreviation

3 *The sound of **-ble** after **SHUN** is represented by* ....⌄........ *joined to the **SHUN hook**, or disjoined* ....⟍.... *written close to the hook:*

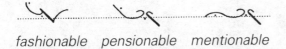

fashionable pensionable mentionable

Progress Check 15.1

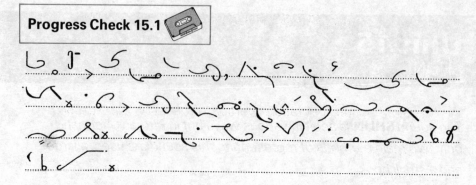

SHUN hook to straight strokes

A large **SHUN hook** at the end of a straight stroke is written:

1 On the opposite side to an initial attachment, to balance the
   outline and keep the stroke straight:

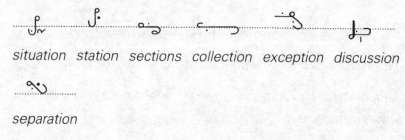

situation station sections collection exception discussion

separation

2 Away from the curve **F,V,L** followed by **K** or **G,** to balance the
   outline and keep the straight stroke straight:

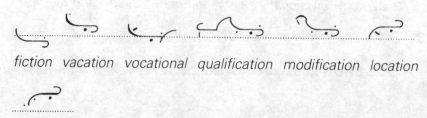

fiction vacation vocational qualification modification location

allegation

3   On the opposite side to the last vowel, as a means of vowel
    indication:

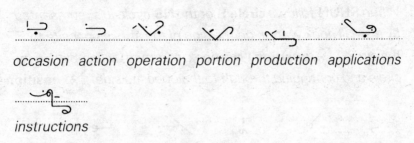

occasion   action   operation   portion   production   applications

instructions

4   On the right-hand side of simple (without attachments) **T, D, J,**
    to keep the forward writing motion:

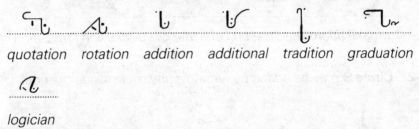

quotation   rotation   addition   additional   tradition   graduation

logician

5   On the same side as an initial hook or circle in some derivatives,
    to enable the following stroke to be written:

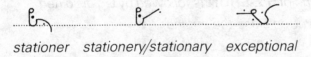

stationer   stationery/stationary   exceptional

Progress Check 15.2

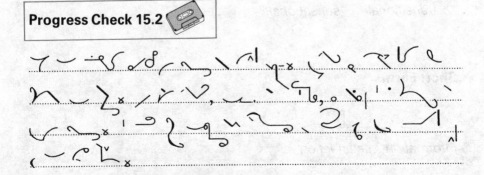

Shun following Circle S or the NS circle

1   When **SHUN** follows **circle S** or the **NS** circle it is represented
    by a small hook written on the side of the stroke opposite to
    the circle, ... **position.** The hook is formed by completing the
    circle and continuing through to the opposite side, ... **position.**

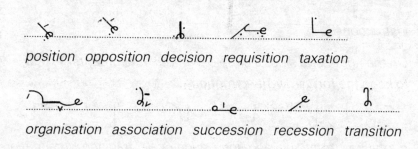

position opposition decision requisition taxation

organisation association succession recession transition

2   **Circle S** may be added by writing a tiny circle inside the hook:

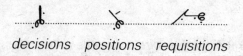

decisions positions requisitions

3   When the sound of **S/Z-SHUN** is followed by **L** a disjoined
    upward L is written close the outline:

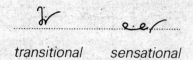

transitional   sensational

Short Forms

information   satisfaction

Intersection

....|.... **attention**

your attention   my attention   attract attention

Phrasing

The large **SHUN hook** *is used to represent the word* **ocean,** *and the small hook to represent the word* **association:**

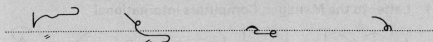

Atlantic Ocean   Pacific Ocean   medical association   your association

Note   *When the sound of* **SHUN** *in the middle of a word is followed by a vowel and* **ST,** *the hook is not used:*

but   *This is an infrequently used rule.*

reception   *receptionist·*

Reading and Writing Practice

1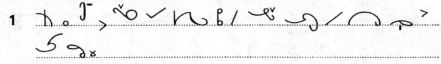

2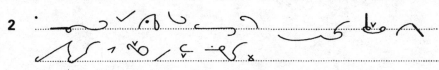

3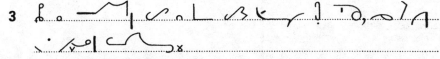

4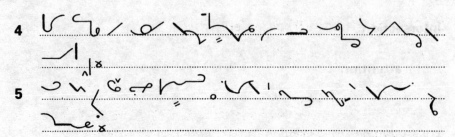

5

Dictation

1 Letter to the Manager, Computers International

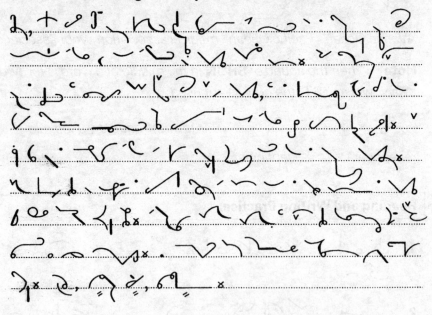

2 Circular letter to all customers

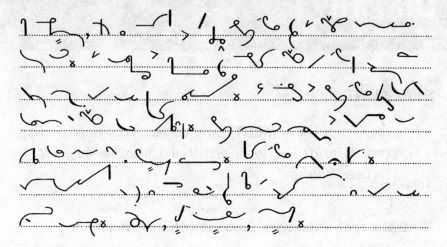

Suffix -MENT

1   As you already know -**MENT** is written ....⌐.... When it is not easy,
    or possible, to join ...⌐. to the end of an outline, half-length **N**
    ...⌐....is used instead:

    department experiment assortment announcement

    pavement adjustment

2   When the root word has a final **hook N** the hook is retained when
    -**MENT** follows, and this is represented by ...⌐.. or ...⌐..., whichever
    is most convenient:

    appointment postponement assignment adjournment

    environment amendment disappointment

Suffix -LY

1   **Stroke L,** joined or disjoined when necessary, plus the third-place
    vowel **i** represents the final sound of -**LY**. It is rarely necessary
    to write the vowel as it is indicated by the stroke. Root outlines
    remain constant:

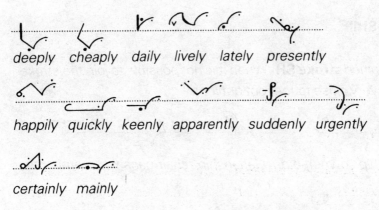

deeply cheaply daily lively lately presently

happily quickly keenly apparently suddenly urgently

certainly mainly

a When a root word ends with **stroke L** or **hook L**, add the
vowel. This is an essential vowel:

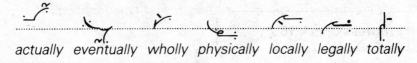

actually eventually wholly physically locally legally totally

Progress Check 16.1

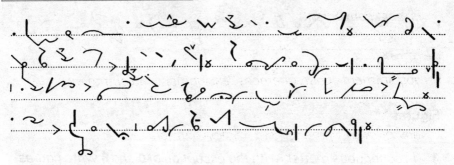

Suffix -ALLY

Write the **hook L** and add the vowel:

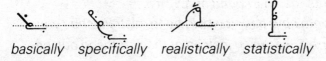

basically specifically realistically statistically

Suffix -SHIP

Add a joined **stroke SH.** *When it is not possible to join the stroke write it very close to the root outline:*

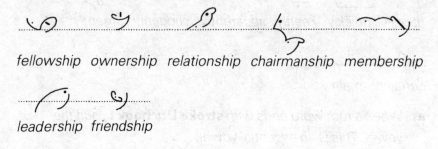

fellowship ownership relationship chairmanship membership

leadership friendship

Progress Check 16.2

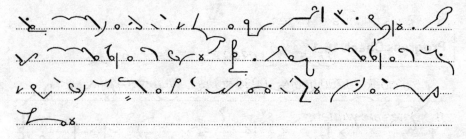

Figures

1 *In continuous matter, with the exception of* **0** *and* **8** *write figures* **1–10,** *and round numbers, in shorthand:*

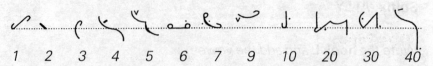

| 1 | 2 | 3 | 4 | 5 | 6 | 7 | 9 | 10 | 20 | 30 | 40 |

You will appreciate how easy it would be to mistranscribe your notes if the figure 6 was used instead of the shorthand outline.

2 *It is safe to represent all other numbers by Arabic numerals:*

   15   24   33   47

15 years   24 metres   33 litres   47 kilometres

3 *Use stroke **N** for **hundred**, **Th** for **thousand** and **M** for **million**:*

   3   5(2   7(9   17 436(5

300   5,200   7,000   9,000,000   17,436,500 tons

4 *Write sums of money as follows, adding **circle S** to **Th** for 'thousand pounds':*

   3   8(4   756. 90   3   2(5

£3,000   £8,400   £756.90 $200 $2,500

5 *Times of day are written:*

   5.   17   0930   7   6

5 o'clock   1700 hours   0930 hours   7 a.m.   6 p.m.

6 *Dates are written:*

   1   22   7(

1 January   1st February   2nd March   22nd July   7th April

   23   21)

23rd May   21st June

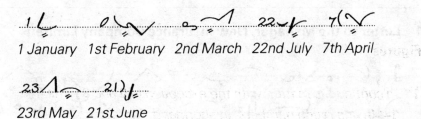

Short Forms

acknowledgement   enlargement

Reading and Writing Practice

Dictation

1 Letter to the Manager, New Insurance Company Limited

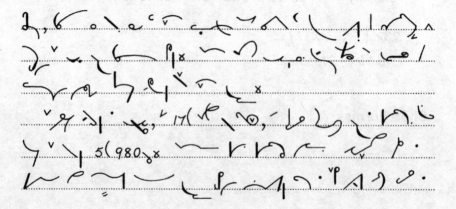

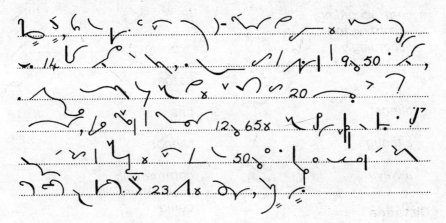

2 Letter to Mr G R Bond, Studio Interiors, Newcastle upon Tyne

Short Forms

*Examples of **some** common derivatives are shown indented.*

a/an		are	
able to		as/has	
accord/according/		be	
according to			
accordingly		being	
all		before	
almost		but	
although		cannot	
always		commercial/	
also		commercially	
altogether		could	
an/a		dear	
and		difficult	
any/in		difficulty	
anybody		do	
anyhow		doing	
anyone		dollar/had	
anything		enlarge	
		enlarged	

enlargement		immediately	
enlarger		in/any	
enlarges		influence	
enlarging		influenced	
eye/I		influencing	
first		influential	
for		information	
from		is/his	
gentleman		it	
gentlemen		its	
had/dollar		January	
has/as		knowledge	
have		acknowledge	
having		acknowledgement	
he (phrasing only)		acknowledging	
his/is		large	
hour/our		largely	
hours/ours		larger	
how		largest	
I/eye		manufacture	
immediate		manufactured	

manufacturer		put	
manufactures		puts	
manufacturing		putting	
more		responsible/ responsibility	
Mrs		satisfaction	
nevertheless		satisfactory	
nothing		unsatisfactory	
notwithstanding		several	
of		shall	
on		should	
ought		something	
our/hour		subject	
ours/hours		subjected	
ourselves		subjecting	
owe/oh		subjects	
owed		thank	
owes		thanked	
owing		thankful	
particular		thanking	
particularly		thanks	
particulars		that	

the (tick used in phrasing)	.	trading	
there/their		two, too	
therefore		unsatisfactory	
thing		very	
anything		we	
nothing		which	
something		who	
think		will	
thinking		willing	
thinks		with	
this		without	
to		wonderful/ wonderfully	
today		would	
tomorrow		year	
to be		yesterday	
together		you	
too/two		your	
trade/toward		yours	
trader		yourself	
trades/towards			

Intersections

Figures in brackets indicate the unit in which that intersection is found:

arrange/arranged/
  arrangement
  arranging (**7**)

attention (**15**)

business (**3**)

charge (**2**)

company (**2**)

company limited (**10**)

corporation (**8**)

department (**1**)

enquire/enquiry/
  inquire/inquiry (**9**)

form (**6**)

month (**5**)

require/required/
  requirement (**7**)

Circle S may be added to the intersections to indicate plurals or possessive case.